Zealous The Zebra And Family

Beginners Reading Book

Stacy M. Brown

Introduction

This story is about zebras and multiple families. It is about teaching the children how to identify their numbers, colors, shapes, count and spell.

Note for Librarians: A cataloguing record for this book is available from Library and Archives
Canada at www.collectionscanada.ca/amicus/index-e.html
ISBN 978-1-4251-2350-5

Printed in Victoria, BC, Canada. Printed on paper with minimum 30% recycled fibre.
Trafford's print shop runs on "green energy" from solar, wind and other environmentally-friendly power sources.

Offices in Canada, USA, Ireland and UK

Book sales for North America and international:
Trafford Publishing, 6E–2333 Government St.,
Victoria, BC V8T 4P4 CANADA
phone 250 383 6864 (toll-free 1 888 232 4444)
fax 250 383 6804; email to orders@trafford.com
Book sales in Europe:
Trafford Publishing (UK) Limited, 9 Park End Street, 2nd Floor
Oxford, UK OX1 1HH UNITED KINGDOM
phone +44 (0)1865 722 113 (local rate 0845 230 9601)
facsimile +44 (0)1865 722 868; info.uk@trafford.com
Order online at:
trafford.com/07-0738

10 9 8 7 6 5 4 3 2

Hi! I'm Zealous the zebra!

I have 1 red single stripe and one red single circle.

Hello! We are the 2 double trouble twin zebras!

We have 2 blue stripes and two blue squares.

Hi! We are the 3 triplet zebras!

We have 3 orange stripes and
three orange stars.

Hello! We are the 4 quadruplet zebras!

We have 4 green stripes and four green rectangles.

Hi! We are the 5 quintuplet zebras!

We have 5 yellow stripes and five yellow ovals.

Hello! We are the 6 sextuplet zebras!

We have 6 brown stripes and six brown triangles.

Hi! We are the 7 septuplet zebras!

We have 7 pink stripes and seven pink hearts.

Hello! We are the 8 octuplet zebras!

We have 8 black stripes and eight black octagons.

Hi! We are the 9 nonuplet zebras!

We have 9 purple stripes and nine purple semi-circles.

Hello! We are the 10 decaplet zebras!

We have 10 white stripes and
ten white diamonds.

Zebra Barn Colors

Zebra Barn Numbers

Zebra Barn Shapes

semi-circle

triangle

square

heart

octagon

oval

star

rectangle

circle

diamond

15

VOCABULARY LIST

A	four	oval	stars	zealous
And	green	pink	six	zebras
Are	have	purple	stripes	
Barn	hearts	quadruplet	ten	
Black	hello	quintuplet	the	
Blue	hi	rectangles	three	
Brown	I	red	triangles	
Circle	nine	semi-circles	triplet	
Colors	nonuplet	septuplets	trouble	
Decaplet	numbers	seven	twins	
Diamonds	octagon	sextuplet	two	
Double	octuplet	shapes	we	
Eight	one	single	white	
Five	orange	squares	yellow	

About the Author/Illustrator:

Stacy M. Brown is a writer, wife, mother and Day Care Provider. She wrote her first book, Zealous The Zebra And Family, because it was a class project. Although, she had always wanted to write books, the 90 Clock Hour CDA course just inspired her to go forth. It is now her desire to continue writing for the children, encouraging, teaching, and inspiring them forevermore with her present and future books to come.